GREAT BIBLE STORIES
JOSEPH IN EGYPT

Adapted by Maxine Nodel   **Illustrated by Norman Nodel**

BARONET BOOKS is a registered trademark of Playmore Inc., Publishers
and Waldman Publishing Corp., New York, N.Y.

Copyright © MCMXCIII Playmore Inc., Publishers
and Waldman Publishing Corp., New York, New York

All Rights Reserved.

BARONET BOOKS, NEW YORK, NEW YORK
Printed in China

During seven years of rich harvests in Egypt, Joseph knew a famine would follow. He stored grain in huge granaries. Soon, people from many lands came to buy grain. Among those were Joseph's brothers who didn't recognize him, but he recognized them!

Joseph greeted his brothers.
"Where are you from?" he asked.
"We come from Canaan. We are brothers," they replied.

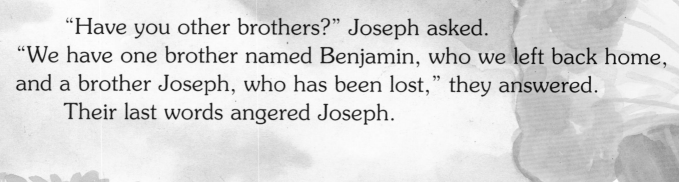

"Have you other brothers?" Joseph asked.
"We have one brother named Benjamin, who we left back home, and a brother Joseph, who has been lost," they answered.
Their last words angered Joseph.

"You are spies!" shouted Joseph. "One of you must remain here as a hostage, while the others can return home. If you come back with your youngest brother you will prove you are not spies."

So the brothers returned to Canaan. But one brother, Simeon, stayed behind in prison.

Back in Canaan, the brothers told Israel, their father, that
they must return to Egypt with Benjamin.

"I have already lost Joseph. I will not let Benjamin go," Israel
cried out.

But soon all their grain was finished.

"Take your brother Benjamin to Egypt, pay double for the grain, but just bring my little one home," ordered Israel. "Let nothing bad befall my youngest son, for that would send me to my grave."

In Egypt, Joseph heard that the men from Canaan had returned, so he ordered Simeon to be released and had his brothers returned to the palace.

When the brothers arrived at the palace, they presented Benjamin to Joseph.

Joseph looked upon Benjamin and said, "May God be gracious to you."

Soon servants set out meat and bread and wine for all the brothers.

But as they ate happily, Joseph spoke to his servant.

"Have all their sacks filled with grain," said Joseph. "But in the sack of Benjamin, place my silver goblet."

Early the next morning, the brothers gathered all their sacks and left for Canaan.

Just as they were about to leave the city, one of Joseph's servants called to them.

"Stop, you can not return to Canaan yet. One of you has stolen my master's silver goblet!"

"That is a lie!" shouted the brothers as they revealed the contents of their sacks.

The servants began searching each of their sacks. He started with the eldest and finally removed the silver goblet from the sack of the youngest, Benjamin.

"Behold!" shouted the servant. "The thief."

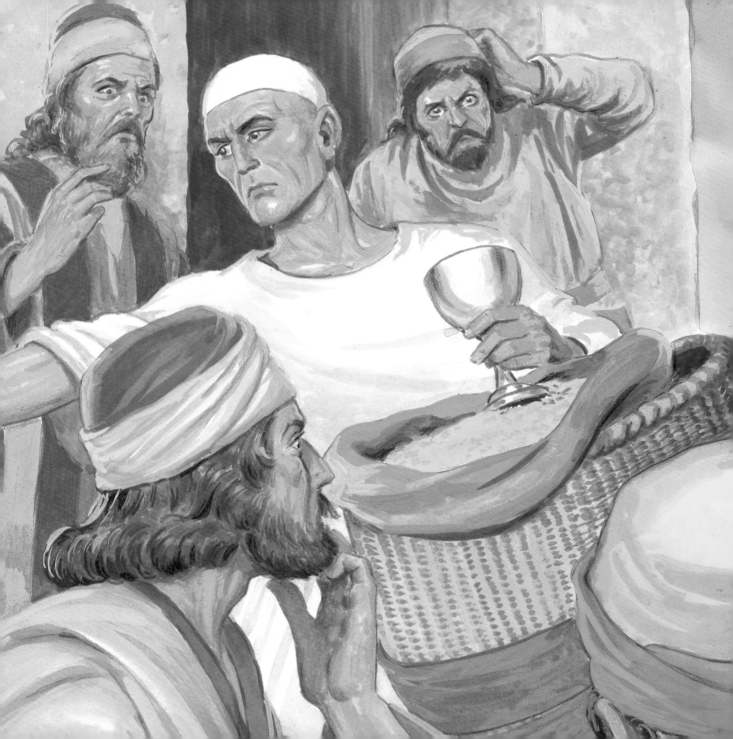

The brothers were taken back to the palace and Joseph ordered that Benjamin be made a slave.

"The rest of you may return to Canaan," said Joseph.

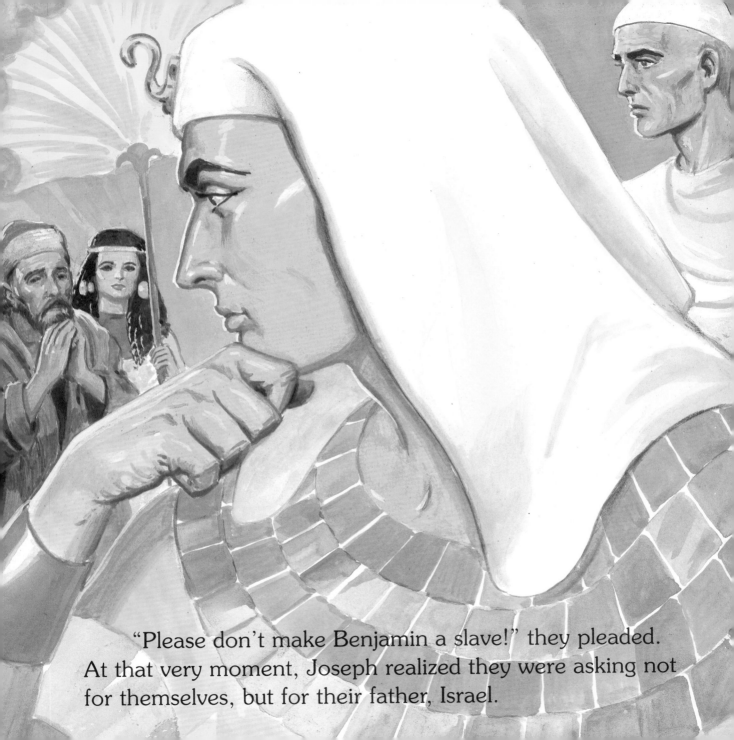

"Please don't make Benjamin a slave!" they pleaded. At that very moment, Joseph realized they were asking not for themselves, but for their father, Israel.

"It is true," said one brother, Judah.
"When our father learns that Benjamin has been made a
slave, he will surely die."

Suddenly Joseph felt much pity for his brothers.
He called to his servants,
"Leave us alone at once!"

Joseph began to weep and revealed his identity
to his brothers.

"I am your brother, Joseph, the one you sold into bondage."

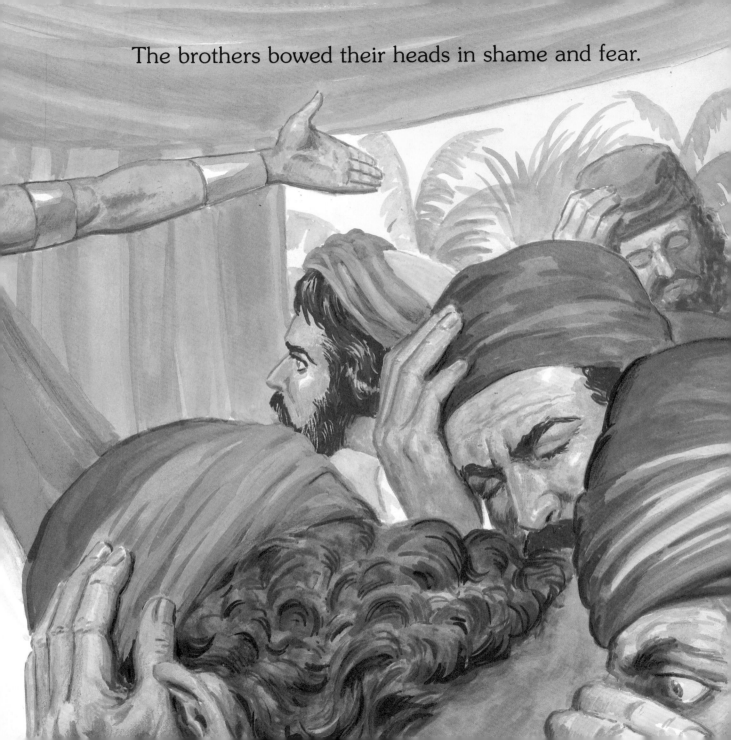

The brothers bowed their heads in shame and fear.

"Be not angry or grieved with yourselves," said Joseph. "For God sent me to Egypt to preserve all of our lives. Rise and go back to Canaan!

Tell our father all that has happened and return here with him and all of our household.

You and Israel shall live in this land and be fed."

So it was that God moved Israel and his children
into the land of Egypt.
And God continued to watch over them all.